The *Perfect* HOme

Valérie,

Tout ce que tu as fait pour Grange !.
incroiable.
Amitiés,
Joe Carroll
juin '03

The Perfect Home

Living In Style
by Joseph Carroll

Copyright© 2001 Furniture/Today

Cahners Business Information, a division of Reed Elsevier, Inc.

All Rights Reserved

All rights reserved. No part of this book may be reproduced in any form without written permission of the copyright owners. All images in this book have been reproduced with the knowledge and prior consent of the artists concerned and no responsibility is accepted by producer, publisher or printer for any infringement of copyright or otherwise arising from the contents of this publication. Every effort has been made to ensure that credits accurately comply with information supplied.

Published by The Ashley Group

A Cahners© Business Information Company

1350 East Touhy Avenue

Des Plaines Illinois 60018

Printed in China

Concept and Design by Dianne Daly Barham

The Daly Group, Kernersville, NC

ISBN 1-58862-085-9

First Edition

Dedication

To my lovely wife Hodges,
whose creative balance of our
individual styles makes our house
a Perfect Home.

22

23

2.

30

4

45

62

94

112

115

Contents

Introduction

"The perfect home is a place to relax, share, party, create, sleep, and be intimate. As Auntie Mame said, 'Life's a banquet and most people are starving to death.' The perfect home lets you live to your fullest."

Raymond Waites

If you are taking the time to look through this book, it's probably because you are curious. Intrigued by the title, The Perfect Home. You may be looking for a certain piece of furniture to purchase or just decorating ideas. You may want to create "the perfect home" to entertain friends or business acquaintances. Or, you may just want to see what you can do to find a few more elements of perfection that will enhance your home.

To help define "the perfect home" we will seek inspiration from furniture designers, decorators, showroom designers and other industry specialists who, for the most part, are not household names. Even though a few have received public recognition, they are well known and well respected by those of us in the home furnishings industry.

The perfect home defines who you are. It's both a retreat and an expression of your personality. It's a place you miss when you're away. It's a place where you love to entertain and where you and your guests can put your feet up and be comfortable. No matter how formal the styling, your furniture should be livable and make you feel relaxed.

What you choose for your home reflects your tastes and thoughts. The key elements are style, personality, color and nature. But the "magic" occurs when these elements work together in concert. We want our home to be beautiful and its interior to reflect our passion. As one designer expressed it, "When I walk into a person's home, the interior should be a feast for the eyes. The furniture, fabrics and colors should work together to create an entertaining, stimulating environment." Or as another put it, "It should make the visitor feel welcome and the owner proud."

Style

"As the perfect home should always reflect the changing lifestyles of its inhabitants, its style will continue to develop. Style is not static. It is a constantly redefining organism reflective of those it shelters."

Howard Greenstein

Style is your signature; it is the "emotional temperature" of your home. Style is about impact. Style is about individuality; it is about assembling things together that are a bit unexpected. It may be adventurous or grandiose, individually unique or romantic, elegantly familiar, simplistic or perfectly sleek.

Style is that certain presence that is difficult to define. It projects your needs, wishes and desires. It's like "star quality"; you know it when you see it.

Left: Southwood–Animal Skin Collection

Style

Create an adventurous style with furniture reminiscent of grand manors or country estates ... where weekend activities included a pheasant shoot or fox hunt. Make up your own "wild" environment by combining a zebra skin rug with a classic European chaise. Or, accent the room with a console that steals its legs from the cypress tree.

... a motif that "turns on" the owner and then is executed with flair and good taste.

Joe Richardson II

... an interpretation of the residents' lifestyle, travels and preferences.

Shirley Goff

For me, "the perfect home" is one that provides its owners a place to retreat from the world and let go. The "perfect home" is one that you miss when you're away and revel in when you return. It is perfectly suited to your taste, your lifestyle, and your sense of aesthetics. It is a creative endeavor in perpetual motion ... a work in progress.

Karyl Pierce Paxton

Left: Harden—Bristol Channel Collection Sleigh Bed
Upper Right: Lloyd/Flanders—Mathias Chaise
Lower Right: Wright Table—Cypress Console Collection

Be grandiose with a French banquet table or elegant with a hand carved English sideboard. Or, escape to the islands with an exotic bamboo and rattan bed.

One should "collect" fine furniture and each piece should invoke a great memory or story.

Charles Sutton

Pieces that can stand on their own but prefer not to.

Sally Altizer

Previous: EJ Victor—Boracay Collection Rattan Bed
Left: EJ Victor—Plume Dining Table—Newport Historic Collection
Right: Marge Carson—Huntington Manor Sideboard

The perfect home is eclectic ... a mixture of a lot of different periods ... the beauty of the old masters, the comfort of tradition that blends so well with contemporary styling, fabrics, materials and colors.

Joe Mallison

Style refers to the historical reference of the home, either traditional or contemporary/modern which generally will in turn dictate the décor. My favorite interior designers, however, would flip the styles to create some excitement; ie, if you have a really great classical background, there would be nothing to stop one from using great modern furnishings as a juxtaposition.

John Mascheroni

Personal style is created out of individual creative and emotional needs, fantasies and lifestyles.

Leatrice Eiseman

Left: Harden–Bristol Channel Scroll Bed
Upper Right: Wright Table–Mackintosh Three Legged Round Table
Lower Right: Southwood–Historic New England Collection

"Romantic" takes us back to the turn of the century opulence of a Newport summer cottage like Rosecliff (1902). Rich velvets and toiles, topiaries, carved tables and oversized floral arrangements enhance the mood.

Style is an indefinable mysterious element that permeates every visual moment of our lives, an elusive quality that evolves and changes. Style evolves from dreams, hopes and desires.

Maria Agnelli

Style is the look that a piece of furniture creates. The combination of elements that blends to make the piece unique.

Jackie Brezney

Left: EJ Victor–Rosecliff Sofa–Newport Historic Collection
Right: EJ Victor–Rosecliff Center Table–Newport Historic Collection

Style

Rich elegant floor coverings, sensual shapes in furniture, intimate vignettes that bring out the romantic in you.

The design and functionality of furniture should represent the style and taste level of the owners. Art and accessories should represent the personality of the owners.

Don Bogish

Lower Left: Masland–Grand Manor Floral Kirman
Center: EJ Victor–Three Chairs–Conversation Seating
Lower Right: Marge Carson–Huntington Manor Bed

*The bedroom often expresses the
owner's romantic view of life.*
Karl Felperin

Familiarity has its "roots" in classic designs. Traditional woods such as mahogany and cherry establish the character and heritage of their setting.

... a look that is both timeless and timely.
Sally Altizer

... is a determinant of perceived value, or appreciation of its basic essence. It reflects and describes beauty and harmony in the aesthetic.
George Kosinski

Upper Left: Wright Table–Mahogany Bow Front Chest
Lower Left: Wright Table–Mahogany Round Pedestal Table
Right: Stickley–Secretary

A perfect home puts a smile on your face when you walk in the door.
Sid Lenger

Wood furniture should be thought of as functional sculpture.
Charles Sutton

Left: Stickley—Classical Inlay Sideboard
Right: Southwood—Jacobean Loveseat

Style

Style is a collection of things that are really loved by their owners ... furnishings that people feel comfortable with ... taking simple things and making them elegant.

Leonard Eisen

Lower Left: Wright Table–French Round Table
Center: Harden–Natural Transitions Collection Bed
Lower Right: Wright Table–Custom Game Table

Style is a synthesis of aesthetic knowledge, spatial sensitivy, personal background/experience and physical needs composed into an environment that provides beauty, pleasure, function and inspiration.

Haig Khachatoorian

If the style is contemporary/modern, the statement is simpler, with a calming effect of quietness. It is not "temporary" but includes a chasteness that has longevity built in from select touches of the past and present.

O B Solie

Bravado shows here. The furniture can invite a "feet up" or "dress for dinner" aura. Perhaps different rooms and areas can provide both, with a movable ambiance for different occasions.

Shirley Goff

Left: American Leather—Tiffany Collection
Upper Right: American Leather—Cloud Nine Collection
Lower Right: Marge Carson—Credenza & Mirror

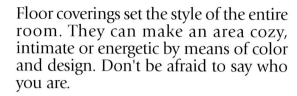

Floor coverings set the style of the entire room. They can make an area cozy, intimate or energetic by means of color and design. Don't be afraid to say who you are.

The whole combination of furniture, accessories, carpet, rugs, etc. that a person ends up with automatically expresses the personality of the owner.
Carrie Bleile

Style is a signature that sets one apart from what is ordinary or expected, yet is visually comfortable and inviting.
D. Michael Gohman

Left: Masland–Custom Swirl Inlaid Rug
Right: Masland-Custom Geometric Inlaid Rug

Personality

"Your furniture says a lot about who you are and what your personality is. Formal, casual, daring, whimsical, fun, stuffy ... each personality trait can be indicated by one's furniture. Expect your friends and guests to make subtle judgements about you based on the way your home is furnished and decorated."

Dudley Moore

Your home is a visual definition of your personality. It shows whether you like to entertain often or whether you prefer it to be your personal sanctuary. It's a place where you can show off your artwork, pottery and other collectibles. It may be a bit cluttered, but it's an accurate reflection of your lifestyle ... on the go with very little time to organize your surroundings. Still, it's a place you're glad to come home to.

Your personality is reflected in your preferences such as wood finishes, colors, textures, fabric and carpet patterns, accessories and family heirlooms. Just like a person, every piece of furniture has a story. The key is to connect yourself with your furniture so that it knows the extension and amplification of your personality.

Casual vs. Formal, Period vs. Contemporary ... furniture provides us with a range of options that allows us to express many personalities throughout the home. It more easily reflects a personality than creates one.

Left: Stickley-Directoire Collection Breakfront Buffet

A home filled with obviously well worn books or personally produced artwork or collections of strange but interesting things tells us that there are interesting people in this house.

Roger Schneeman

One could say that the room is a canvas and the furniture the paint ... thus a work of art. "Show me your friends and I will tell you who you are." So, show me your furnishings.

James DiPersia

The happiest homes, homes where the people in them thrive, are homes that evoke the personality of the homeowners. Your home is a reflection of you, who you are, your style. Without that imprint, a home is simply a box with stuff.

Sandra Goodall

Previous: Harden–Upholstery and Tapestry Collection
Left: Marge Carson–Bellagio Gentleman's Chest
Right: EJ Victor–Carol Hicks Bolton Collection Sofa

The books you read or collect and display express your personality to others. It's always fun to leave a book open at a certain place for a guest to read or view a picture that sets the mood you wish to create.

It is important to know and realize that as each person has a unique personality, so does a piece of furniture, fabric or a piece of art. To ignore that aspect of furniture, whether old or new, is to leave out the most enjoyable part of buying and owning furniture.

Sid Lenger

Left: EJ Victor–Breakfront China
Right: Southwood–Transitional Sofa & Traditional Chair

Your furniture should express your true personality, the "you" that you like best. Use your choices to define yourself and for the benefit of communicating to others.

Alexander Julian

A person is most at peace when the things surrounding them reflect who they are. For example, a person who likes classical music, opera and dressy clothes will be more at home with shiny, dressy fabrics. A person who likes stockcar racing would be at home with a vinyl recliner with a cooler in the arm.

Richard Bennington

Left: Marge Carson–Bellagio Collection Display Cabinet
Right: Southwood–English Arm Sofa & Leather Cocktail Ottoman

Personality

Personality like this is not limited to just old and antique furniture. Through patient searching and enjoyment of the process of selecting and connecting, each piece of furniture can fill not only the spot in your home but also a place in your soul to become part of your personality and heritage.

Sid Lenger

Furniture (as art) can be the window to our soul. Furniture and accessories express our personality.

Bob Timberlake

Everyone has his or her own style. If they open up and let their personalities show through in their living environments, they will have created the perfect home.

Joe Richardson III

Previous: Harden–Forbes Collection Chateau Dining Table
Left: Marge Carson–Casetta Collection Display Case
Right: EJ Victor–Chinoiserie Sideboard–Newport Historic Collection

Personality

Southern hospitality is personified here with a cherry plantation bed while the den eloquently defines a New England heritage. These rooms instantly convey the personality of their owners.

Personal style, function, arrangement, level of concinnity and eclecticism ... color and color combinations, textures, materials, how furniture is displayed, all express your personality.

Walt Shaw

All pieces would look as if they were well worn, by time and use. This (to me) would create a perfectly inviting, yet stylish, atmosphere.

Jon Willis

Left: Harden–Classic Cherry Collection Plantation Bed
Right: Southwood–Historic New England Collection

Personality

A den Mission oak, an "Easy Chair" by the window, a cozy mountain retreat all say welcome, come stay a while, we're very friendly.

While there is probably no such thing as a perfect home, if your home reflects your values and you enjoy living there, it is your perfect home for now. Your home, its furnishings, colors, materials and artifacts should be the product of your interests, hobbies and vocation.

Roger Schneeman

The perfect home is where people live surrounded by things they like and that make them comfortable. It's as simple as that.

Billy Baldwin

The perfect home should be about all the things that you love in an atmosphere where you can be yourself.

Leonard Eisen

Left: Stickley–Spindle Settle Group
Right: Stickley–Tufted Chair & Ottoman
Next Page: Lloyd Flanders-Heritage Seating

Light & Color

"Light is harvested through windows, lighting fixtures and fireplaces. It is reflected from the walls, floors, furnishings and people's faces to produce the mood, the very spirit of an environment. Nothing is more important."

Roger Schneeman

Light and color set the mood of a room. It can be bright and airy, energetic, soothing and relaxing, or dramatic and exciting. Important sensory effects happen when light and color are utilized to add mood to any room setting. They are the key definers of space. They accent the individual pieces of furniture in the room and define its mood. They also have an effect on the mood of its occupants.

Without light there is no color. Light, both natural and artificial, can be manipulated with color to offer an infinite variety of moods within a setting. Among them a sense of joy, tranquility, sensuality and well being. Light and color create emotions and desires ... what comfort level do I need ... warm, cuddly and fuzzy or upbeat and passionate? Light and color are animators. It's exciting to see unusual colors working together in harmony.

Left: Marge Carson–Huntington Manor Collection Armoire

Light and color are critical to the home because they accentuate or camouflage everything else.
My personal rule is don't be afraid of color. It is one of the most cost-effective ways to change your home. The use of color and lighting shape your home dramatically from natural light spilling out of a window to a simple bedside lamp. Lighting and color create the emotional way we experience a room.

Kathy Ireland

I like a natural light filled home. The constantly changing light creates moods and gives the colors punch, evolving with the seasons or each day.

Mike Warren

Previous: Harden—Traditional Sofa & Tapestry Collection Cocktail Table
Left: Masland—Tangier Carpet
Right: EJ Victor—Carol Hicks Bolton Collection Chair

Light & Color

You set the mood of your room by increasing or decreasing the amount of light. Shutters and shades act as filters. Light colors in carpet or upholstery intensify the effect. Hardwood floors reflect light or create a warmth or richness with their wood tones. Decorative mullions not only create interesting window art but can also cast mood setting shadows throughout the room.

Lower Left: Masland–Sea Island Carpet
Center: Marge Carson–Casetta Dining Collection
Lower Right: American Leather–Toscana Collection

Light and color accent the individual pieces in the room and define its mood.

Christopher Natale

It has everything to do with the way people react in a space. My city loft is dark and dramatic ... perfect at night and for parties. In East Hampton the color palette is light and full of light. Different moods for different places and activities.

Raymond Waites

Light and color play important roles when it comes to creating an atmosphere of gracious living ... a sense of warmth and welcome.

Robert Ficks

What sound is to music, light is to design. It's this seemingly non-physical entity that one plays and jousts with. Color is one of the "nets" that is used to capture light.

Vaida Daukautas

Previous: Masland–Kashmir Carpet
Left: Marge Carson–Venetian Style Dining
Right: EJ Victor–Dining Table with White Damask Fabric Chairs

Along with the correct color, light can be used to open up an area, making it fresh and inviting. At the same time, the use of light and color reflects on the personal furnishings of a room.

Philip Martin

Light and color play an important part in home décor. For a restful environment, choose cool colors. If you are avant guard, use bright colors, like red.

Don Taylor

Left: Masland–Custom Scroll Inlaid Rug
Right: American Leather–Bianco Collection

I like to walk into a room and see unusual colors working together beautifully. And, as I gaze into the next room, and the next, I like all the colors in the house to have harmony.

Dudley Moore

The role that light and color play in the home is one of the most important elements of design and is perhaps the most ignored. Both light and color have tremendous impacts on our psyche and sense of well being in different ways and at different times in our lives. Attaining an awareness of how light and color affects us as an individual is a huge step in not only creating a home that is a comfortable refuge but also an insight into ourselves.

Karyle Pierce Paxton

Upper Left: Wright Table–Freestanding Legs Table
Lower Left: American Leather–Weekender Collection
Right: American Leather–Kendall Collection

Yellow can make a strong statement or a subtle one. Light can give it energy – or a calming effect. When choosing color be sure to look at it in all lighting conditions: daylight, candlelight, direct and indirect.

Lighting should consider the overall room. Accent with rheostats. Color creates a mood, but exact matching, I believe, is passe and boring. Both light and color should be considered in both daytime and evening atmosphere.
Shirley Goff

Color is the most important element to convey style. Color expresses all emotions ... calm or electric, basic or rich, light or dark. Lighting brings drama into an environment. Paint a room with light to accent the positive.
Raymond Waites

Previous: American Leather–Zurich Collection
Left: Southwood–Louis XV French Settee
Right: Masland–Creare/Cut Pile Loop Carpet

Family & Friends

"I know my house is right when I can't get people to leave. If a home is furnished with friends and family in mind, it is the place where people gather, stay and never quite want to say goodnight."
Sandra Goodall

Your family and friends want your home to express your personality, not just the latest trends. One way to bring the family closer is to start collecting pieces of furniture when your children are young. As they grow up with the furniture, they feel a connection. Over time you will see these pieces reinvented, surrounded by newer accents or pieces of art, just by changing the room arrangement and by innovative juxtaposition of design and color.

Your home exudes your tastes, lifestyle and personal moods to others without you saying a word. It should be inviting and comfortable, not a museum. Furnishings have a tremendous effect on your family and friends. Furniture should be pre-arranged in groups that spark conversation and promote ease of movement. Chairs talk to sofas, sofas to chairs and ottomans. A chair can say, "Relax, put your feet up and be at home." Or it can say, "Be careful. Don't sit here. Don't mess me up."

Left: Harden—Retro Group Platform Bed

Decorate the guest room with a travel or exotic location theme. Create a storybook setting. Your friends will enjoy experiencing a taste of your lifestyle.

The bedroom is where you can be more individualistic – let the area and furnishings reflect the personality of the residents.

Carl Grohs, Jr.

Left: Stickley–Sleigh Bed
Right: Harden–Tapestry Collection Monogram Iron Bed

The sofa sleeper can be a stylish addition to the guest room, a city loft or a small apartment. It's a personable way to welcome family and friends.

Love. Good energy. Less is more. You don't have to have lots of money or a big fancy space to have a perfect home.

Rick Lee

Previous: Harden–Shaker Mission Group Twin Beds
Left: American Leather–Comfort Sleeper By Night
Right: American Leather–Comfort Sleeper By Day

*If you like to entertain family and
friends, pieces should be welcoming.
Furniture should be arranged to
enable conversation and promote
easy movement.*

Rick Lee

Left: Southwood—Chinese Chippendale Chair
Right: Southwood—Historic New England Living Room

The living room has a tradition of its own. (Unfortunately) many new homes have eliminated this room. To me, the structure of good English or American designs (such as sofa/love), combined with French Baroque chairs and glass top cocktail tables, works.

Joe Mallison

Like many of our friends, our living room is used less than our family room or kitchen/dining room. It serves to display art objects, art furniture, paintings. It is a focal point upon entering our home.

Mark Singer

Left: Southwood–Traditional Camel Back Sofa
Right: American Leather–Santiago Collection

The perfect home reflects the whole family. Today, families are making choices together and as our lifestyles evolve so do our family's needs. I believe comfort is the main ingredient in creating a distinctive home. It is no longer a trend, it's a revolution. Families no longer just ask for it, but they demand it.

Kathy Ireland

Previous: EJ Victor—Boracay Collection Sofa
Left: Masland—Mixed Textures Custom Inlaid Rug
Right: Stickley—Metropolitan Dining Collection

The dining room is a great place for ritual gathering, such as during the holidays and special occasions.

Rick Lee

Lower Left: Wright Table–Bowfront Server
Center: Stickley–18th Century Dining Room
Lower Right: Wright Table–Country English Sideboard
Next Page: Marge Carson–Huntington Manor Collection

The classics: large seating, beautiful woods & veneers. Comfortable chairs for periods of time for discussion and conversations.

Joe Mallison

Living with Nature

*"Every home has windows that reflect the environment so nature
must invariably be a presence. Whether the glowing sunset hues and
blooming cacti colors set against the neutral sandy shades of the
southwestern desert, the ever present cedar greens and deep lake blues
of the Pacific Northwest, or the sophisticated blacks, skyscraper grays
and twilight teals of an urban landscape, nature is omnipresent."*

Leatrice Eiseman

Nature is perfect. So the perfect home acknowledges that truth. By selecting textures, colors and shapes from nature, the perfect home finds ways to bring the outdoors in. Nature is reflected throughout the home ... beautiful woods and natural materials, organic shapes and colors. These natural elements are combined in furniture to create visually stimulating pieces.

All design begins with nature. When bringing nature indoors through the use of viewing areas, we add an air of openness. Nature's colors and elements tend to relax and comfort. Our home is part of its outside environment. Ours is not a house on the hill ... it's a house of the hill. A house is stark and naked without nature. A house needs a home as well ... that home is nature.

Left: Lloyd Flanders—Embassy Daybed

Living with Nature

More and more we are opening our homes to the outdoors ... playing to private gardens and open living spaces.

Joe Ruggiero

The table should be round or square, so you can get a little "crossfire" conversation going.

Sally Altizer

"The perfect home" can be rooted in a natural way to bring the outdoors in. Selecting textures, colors and shapes from nature can come from wallpaper or dimensional growths.

O B Solie

Left: Harden–Tapestry Collection
Right: Brown Jordan–Havana Collection

Living with Nature

Nature is shared when we hang a sailboat picture from the lakehouse or display our collection of botanical prints. Nature's creatures, like the butterfly, bring grace and beauty to any room.

The perfect home is where your heart is and your treasure ... a place that brings you pleasure, joy and comfort. It's timeless and alive. A place that makes you feel good and inspired and happy.

Bob Timberlake

Lower Left: Lloyd Flanders—Embassy Lounge Chair & Ottoman
Center: EJ Victor—Carol Hicks Bolton Collection Wing Chair
Lower Right: Brown Jordan—East Lake Collection Chair

*Nature means peace and serenity.
Bringing nature indoors through the
use of viewing areas adds an air of
openness. By adding nature's colors
and elements, the space tends to relax
and comfort the spirit.*
Darrell Lowman

Living with Nature

The umbrella can be more than strictly functional in an outdoor setting. It can also be used to create a mood—for privacy during your morning brunch—or, for a festive evening meal just by stringing mini-lights along the stretchers.

I always strive to use nature. It reawakens our senses, such as touch, feel and smell. Some of the most beautiful homes I have encountered are those that celebrate the surroundings, local vernacular or vegetation of a geographical region.

Kathy Ireland

Left: Brown Jordan—Provence Collection
Right: Brown Jordan—Tamiami Collection

You are comfortable with using outdoor furniture inside, but imagine the excitement you will create with a traditional inside collection dressed for dinner on the veranda. Step "outside" of the mold for one evening.

Using windows for natural light, and in some cases for viewing large areas of the surrounding grounds, is one way to bring nature through the architecture. Also by porches, decks, etc. The wood species and the finishes of the furniture can easily incorporate nature into the home.

Jason Payton

Previous: Harden–Bristol Channel Collection Trestle Table
Left: Brown Jordan–Havana Collection
Right: Brown Jordan–Day Lily Collection

Living with Nature

The perfect home cannot exist without
an interaction with nature. Nature is
the balance in life, particularly in this
modern world. Without it we can not
obtain a sense of well being. The
perfect home, whether in a city or
provincial setting, will always have
elements of nature ... a water garden
... living plants and flowers ... birds.
Any and all of these not only provide
visual beauty, but they also affect our
sense of sound, smell and touch.

Karyl Pierce Paxton

Lower Left: Brown Jordan—East Lake Collection
Center: Brown Jordan—Legend Collection
Lower Right: Lloyd Flanders—Ibiza Chaise

Just as there must be private areas for me within my home space, there also needs to be a transparent separation between the home and the landscape.

Robert Tiffany

Return to the era of porch entertaining. Side porches and front porches are once again the popular gathering spot. Use them like every other room. Add a floor lamp or a chandelier. Accent with an area rug. Shades you can easily roll down are a great look as well as control over the elements.

The comfort of nature calms the interior and brings a great reference for freshness and clarity.

Michael Delgaudio

Left: Lloyd Flanders–Keepsakes Glider & Rocker
Right: Lloyd Flanders–Reflections

Living with Nature

Glass brings the outdoors in and takes the indoors out. It lets us experience the changes in weather and seasons, the awakening of the morning and the relaxation of the evening.

Roger Schneeman

Nature is the context in which a home resides. There must be an interplay between the outside spaces and the inside spaces that form a living environment, both physically and visually.

Haig Khachatoorian

Previous: Lloyd Flanders–Casa Grande Sectional
Left: Brown Jordan–Aero Dining
Right: Brown Jordan–Futura Outdoor Furniture

Living with Nature

Saturday barbecue, 4 o'clock tea, or an evening soiree. Let Mother Nature be your hostess. It's the "perfect" entertainment style.

The primary reason for most furniture is function; its redemption is harmony in its environment, which is integral with beauty.

George Kosinski

Left: Lloyd Flanders—Heirloom Collection
Right: Stickley—Outdoor Mission Collection Dining

Conclusion

"The perfect home is ever changing ... as we enter into different phases of life, our home changes as well. It grows as we grow."
Dwayne Welch

As you may have guessed by now, there is no "perfect style", no "perfect interior design scheme". The perfect home is a combination of personal style and whatever best suits the style of the home itself. The furniture designers who contributed to this book are very articulate in their belief that the perfect home is always a work in progress ... it is never static, always vibrant and alive. This is because it reflects the interest and personality of its owner. It's a retreat, a sanctuary from the stress of outside pressures. It's a place you don't want to leave in the morning and one you can't wait to get back to at night.

The perfect home is your home ... whatever it is and however you choose to make it so. You are surrounded by the things you like ... things that make you comfortable. It's as simple as that.

Left: Joe and Hodges Carroll

American Leather

Founded in 1990, Dallas-based AMERICAN LEATHER has brought comfort, design and technical innovation to the leather upholstery manufacturing industry. The company's products, delivered in four weeks, are made to order with a choice of 70 styles and 70 colors. Ultrasuede, the ultimate fabric, is available in over 90 colors to compliment the leather selection.

Bringing together contemporary, transitional and traditional furniture designs, the AMERICAN LEATHER line is also available in a wide variety of sizes and pieces. These include sofas, loveseats, chairs, recliners, sleepers and sectionals. All styles are standard with a comprehensive five-year warranty and lifetime warranty on frame and suspension.

The AMERICAN LEATHER STUDIO collection consists of original styles by some of the industry's best-known designers, including Jena Hall, Rick Lee, Vladimir Kagan and John & Mark Mascheroni.

To maximize quality and efficiency in manufacturing, AMERICAN LEATHER combines state-of-the-art technology with hands-on craftsmanship. This allows consumers to select the exact color, style and size that are right for their home and lifestyle without the wait normally associated with custom-made upholstery.

AMERICAN LEATHER has recently expanded its product offerings to include a variety of convertible sofa beds, recliners and motion products.

AMERICAN LEATHER
3700 Eagle Place Drive, Suite 100
Dallas, TX 75236

www.americanleather.com
Tel: 800-456-9599 x 222
Fax: 972-296-8859

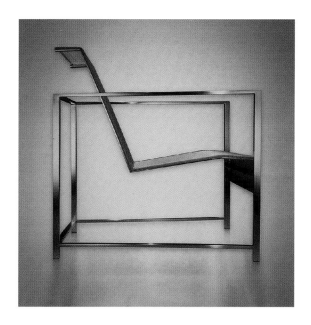

Brown Jordan

Since 1945, BROWN JORDAN has designed luxury leisure furniture. In the early years, renowned furniture designers Bob Brown, Carroll Williams and Hall Bradley all imagined and created collectible furnishings, which are widely sought after and still available today through Brown Jordan.

In 1981, Richard Frinier joined the company's legacy of designers and renewed the company vision with original designs that span architectural styles from modern and contemporary to transitional, traditional and classic. For 20 years, Frinier's expansive design contributions have possessed the unmistakable look that is Brown Jordan.

In 2001, BROWN JORDAN introduced two modern designs constructed in stainless steel, "Nxt" and "Vu." These new classics, inspired by the great architectural styles of the 20th and 21st centuries, present a view of what's next in luxury leisure furnishings.

Over the years, BROWN JORDAN has earned a reputation as a trendsetter in luxury leisure furniture. The Company's unique furnishings are marketed through designer showrooms to the architectural and interior design community, fine furniture stores and select specialty retailers.

BROWN JORDAN's innovative collections are constructed in all-weather materials including stainless steel, powder-coated extruded, cast and wrought aluminum; teak and fine woven resin for full-time outdoor or indoor use. The company's designs accent the indoor and outdoor living spaces of the finest estates, hotels and spas internationally.

BROWN JORDAN continues its legendary design spirit with vision, innovation and expertise.

BROWN JORDAN
9860 Gidley Street
El Monte, CA 91731

www.brownjordan.com
Tel: 626-443-8971
Fax: 626-575-0126

E J Victor

E J VICTOR was founded November 29, 1989 by three former Henredon employees who saw a void in the marketplace for another high-end producer of quality case goods and upholstery. The active principals were Edward W. Phifer III, Joseph B. Manderson, and John Victor Jokinen, hence the name E J VICTOR. Manufacturing facilities are located in Morganton, N.C., geographical center of a strong supply of highly skilled upholstery and woodworking craftsmen. E J VICTOR employs about 300 people and occupies three plants totaling approximately 400,000 square feet.

The company mission statement sums up the spirit and goals of owners and employees: "To satisfy the most selective and knowledgeable consumers with fashionable furniture that is skillfully crafted by dedicated, caring craftsmen, using the finest materials available. Our commitment to value, service, and quality is demonstrated through favorable relationships with our dealers, employees, and suppliers. Our organization's desire is to enhance the quality of life of everyone we touch."

Each piece of furniture is handcrafted to perfection–a reflection of uncompromising standards and attention to detail, both seen and unseen.

E J VICTOR is licensed by The Preservation Society of Newport County, Rhode Island to reproduce the exquisite pieces in the luxurious "summer cottages" of the ultra rich families who lived there such as the Rockefellers, Vanderbilts and Astors. This provides unlimited possibilities for continuing to manufacture the finest and most beautiful antiques of tomorrow for years to come.

E J VICTOR may be purchased through a variety of distributors including furniture stores, chains, interior designers, and "to the trade" design showrooms.

E J VICTOR
110 Wamsutta Mill Road
Morganton, NC 28680

www.ejvictor.com
Tel: 828-437-1991
Fax: 828-438-0744

Harden Furniture

Since 1844, HARDEN FURNITURE has been committed to producing fine, heirloom-quality furniture in a family tradition that has spanned five generations. It is the oldest family-owned furniture manufacturer in the nation and one of the few still privately held. Founded in 1844 as C. Harden & Son, the company is known today as HARDEN FURNITURE, and occupies more than 500,000 square feet of manufacturing facilities in McConnellsville, NY located at the foothills of the Adirondack Mountain region. Their staff includes more than 575 employees, many of whom are expert craftspeople in the art of making furniture. HARDEN manages its own forest preserve–and owns its own sawmill, allowing the greatest possible quality control of materials used to make the company's products. Although mechanization is essential to the manufacturing process, most of the work that goes into producing each finished piece is still done by hand, as it was in Harden's earliest days.

HARDEN produces furniture in a broad range of styles in both solid wood and upholstery–traditional and transitional–to suit every taste. These include 18th century, European, Shaker, Empire and Art Deco-inspired designs. A hallmark of HARDEN FURNITURE is the care and craftsmanship that go into each creation. Through its highly trained and dedicated craftspeople, the company pays strict attention to details that separate Harden Furniture from its competitors in the minds of customers.

Founded on family tradition and community pride, the future of HARDEN FURNITURE can best be described in the company motto: "Fine furniture from generation to generation."

HARDEN FURNITURE
8550 Mill Pond Way
McConnellsville, NY 13401

www.harden.com
Tel: 315-245-1000
Fax: 315-245-2884
email: harden@harden.com

Lloyd Flanders

In 1917, Marshall Burns Lloyd patented a new process for manufacturing wicker furniture. Lloyd realized that the traditional method of painstakingly hand-weaving wicker around individual frames would be almost impossible to mechanize, so he sought to separate the weaving process from the creation of the frame. His newly patented process used looming machines to produce wicker in the form of a pliable, resilient fabric, which was nailed onto bentwood frames and then finished with a braided fiber binding. The mass production of wicker was about to become a reality for the first time.

The Lloyd® Loom was first employed in producing baby carriages. In 1992, Lloyd® Loom introduced their first furniture collection. Lloyd Manufacturing would go on to produce over 10 million pieces in 1,000 designs over the next 18 years. Lloyd® Loom pieces were selected to furnish mansions, hotels, clubs and luxurious ocean liners, as well as the homes of ordinary American citizens.

In 1982, Don Flanders of Flanders Industries, Inc. purchased the original Lloyd Manufacturing facility. A new corporate entity, LLOYD®/FLANDERS, was born. By combining the technology of Mr. Lloyd and the idea of creating wicker furniture for outdoor living, a new category of furniture was created ... All-Weather Wicker.

In 1993, LLOYD®/FLANDERS created LLOYD®/FLANDERS ALUMINUM, a comprehensive collection of extruded and cast aluminum furniture for the pool and patio.

As the creator of All-Weather Wicker, LLOYD®/FLANDERS has enjoyed unprecedented growth, becoming one of the leading manufacturers of premium outdoor furniture in the United States. LLOYD®/FLANDERS employs over 500 and occupies a 500,000 square foot facility in Menominee, Michigan, as well as a 150,000 square foot facility in Ft Smith, Arkansas.

LLOYD®/FLANDERS INDUSTRIES, INC.
3010 10th Street
Menominee, Michigan 49858

www.lloydflanders.com
Tel: 800-526-9894 x 258
Fax: 800-242-6598

Marge Carson

MARGE CARSON is a manufacturer of high-end residential furniture, including upholstery, bedrooms, dining rooms, occasional pieces, and decorative accessories. The company was founded in 1947 by Marjorie Reese Carson, an interior designer who was having trouble finding the right pieces for her California clients. She felt the only way to be sure of getting the types of furnishings she wanted was to build them herself. Consequently, she hired two upholsterers and began making decorative upholstery in a converted chicken coop.

The company soon flourished and embarked on a series of product expansions and improved production facilities. In 1953, the current factory and offices were built on the original site in Rosemead, California, a suburb of Los Angeles.

In 1995, Jim LaBarge purchased MARGE CARSON from Masco Corporation.

MARGE CARSON exemplifies a category of home furnishings distinguished by casual elegance. Most MARGE CARSON designs are rooted in tradition, but are given a contemporary twist through the finish or detailing. The MARGE CARSON look is a combination of style, scale, proportion, finish and fabric all working in harmony. Most pieces are generously scaled and proportioned. Thanks largely to the influence of MARGE CARSON, the overscaled California look has since spread throughout the country. Other features typical of MARGE CARSON Furniture are a mixture of fabrics, materials, textures and decorative finishes that work together to create an ambiance of casual elegance.

MARGE CARSON, INC.
9056 East Garvey Ave.
Rosemead, CA 91770-0889

www.margecarson.com
Tel: (626) 571-1111
Fax: (626) 571-0924

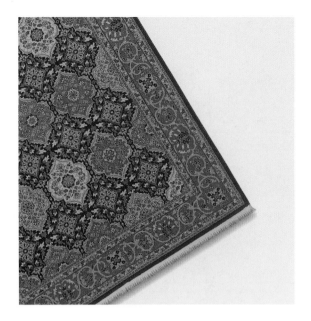

Masland Carpets

Since 1866, MASLAND CARPETS has been designing and producing some of the finest carpets and rugs made in America. Over its 135-year history, the company has gained a reputation for quality, service, and design leadership.

Recognized the world over for its quality craftsmanship, extraordinary colors, and unique designs, MASLAND carpets and rugs grace the floors of countless private residences and exclusive commercial facilities throughout the world.

Well-known celebrities, athletes, and entertainers are among the many high-profile clients MASLAND serves on a regular basis.

MASLAND has recently made significant additions to its area rug design catalog, the MASLAND RUG COLLECTION, thereby continuing to expand its lead in the art of custom inlaid rugs. The comprehensive catalog includes a huge array of new rug patterns, along with numerous popular designs that customers continue to request. The expanded range of styling selections in this edition reflects the diversity now prevalent in interior design, yet the program remains simple and accessible.

Carpets and rugs by MASLAND reflect the value the company places on the individual. In the home, MASLAND's products enable consumers to create an inviting and personalized atmosphere with designs that are tasteful and timeless. Whether traditional or contemporary, each MASLAND design is rendered in only the finest materials, further assuring the customer that the carpet they have selected will stand the test of time.

MASLAND CARPETS
716 Bill Myles Drive
Saraland, AL 36571

www.maslandcarpets.com
Tel: 800-633-0468
Fax: 251-675-5808

Southwood Furniture

SOUTHWOOD represents a rare and unusual step in the making of fine furniture. It all began in 1973 when three individuals, each with successful careers in furniture making, decided to form a "family company" and specialize in what they knew best—the recreation of beautiful upholstered chairs and sofas of the 18th and 19th century periods that led to careful selection of particular patterns with the added dimension of newly-developed skills and improved sense of proportion. There was a desire not only to recreate these treasures, but also to demonstrate that, indeed, excellence still existed in quality and craftsmanship.

The founders of SOUTHWOOD had a vision to become America's premier maker of antique reproductions, as well as traditional upholstered seating, for both residential and hospitality settings. It was decided during the start-up sequence to make each piece with "contract construction standards" to withstand heavy commercial use in fine hotels, country clubs, retirement homes, executive offices and embassies around the world. The development of skirted chairs and sofas and leather upholstery achieves a variety of classical and traditional design choices unequalled in the furniture industry. The Southampton occasional wood division specializes in English reproductions, unique traditional styles and hand-painted pieces.

SOUTHWOOD FURNITURE CORPORATION was acquired in 1994 by four partners who remain committed to the belief that quality and craftsmanship can best be fostered in the intimacy of a small, personal "family company". The key ingredient in every upholstered chair and sofa is still the talent and skill of the individual who creates it. And SOUTHWOOD is especially enriched with some of the furniture industry's most experienced craftsmen. Many are second, third, or fourth generation furniture makers. There are people who care, people who take pride in their profession.

SOUTHWOOD FURNITURE
2860 Nathan Street
Hickory, NC 28602

www.southwoodfurn.com
Tel: 828-465-1776
Fax: 828-465-0858

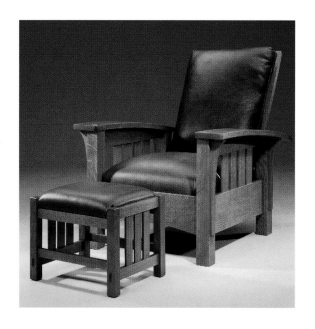

Stickley Furniture

When Leopold Stickley left the Craftsman Shops in Eastwood, New York in 1900, he and his younger brother John George bought the Collin, Sisson & Pratt furniture factory in Fayetteville, New York. Their company, L. & J.G .STICKLEY, was incorporated four years later.

At the Craftsman Shops, Leopold worked for his older brother Gustav who was a major proponent of the Arts and Crafts movement that had created a new aesthetic—one which stressed function and unadorned beauty over the ornateness of the Victorian era.

The new style was championed in America by the likes of the Greene Brothers in California, Frank Lloyd Wright in the Midwest and the Stickley brothers in New York.

L. & J. G. STICKLEY introduced their first furniture line, the Mission Oak, in 1905. Their collection of "simple furniture built along mission lines" was very well received and helped set the standard in fine American woodwork for the entire furniture industry. By the end of World War I the Mission style had lost much of its popularity, but today these pieces are coveted by museums and collectors and bring premium bids at auction.

Experts over the years have recognized STICKLEY's craftsmanship and acclaimed these creations for their purity of form, soundness of construction and fitness of purpose. On January 21, 1956 Leopold Stickley was named "Reverend Dean of Cabinet Makers whose art and craftsmanship has contributed mightily to American home life" by House Beautiful, House & Garden, National Geographic, The New Yorker, Fortune and others.

A new era began for STICKLEY when in 1974 Alfred and Aminy Audi purchased the company and guided it to new levels of accomplishments. Today the company employs over 1,300 artisans and craftspeople. STICKLEY's unwavering commitment to quality craftsmanship remains unchanged. Outstanding design, integrity of construction and the quest for perfection in every aspect is akin to Gustav Stickley's motto, "Als ik kan" which loosely translated means "to the best of my ability".

STICKLEY FURNITURE
1 Stickley Drive
Manlius, NY 13104

www.stickley.com
Tel: 315-682-5500
Fax: 315-682-6306

Wright Table Company

WRIGHT TABLE COMPANY shipped its first furniture November 15, 1971, from a small rented building in Morganton, North Carolina. There were three employees.

In 1976 WRIGHT TABLE COMPANY moved its finishing and shipping operations to Chesterfield, five miles northeast of Morganton. In 1981 the remainder of the operation was moved to a newer expanded facility. The company now had twenty-two employees.

Owner Don Wright has the following to say about this company:

"The WRIGHT TABLE COMPANY is not at the forefront of anything. Our company does not attempt to educate the public. We assume, rightly or wrongly, that you know what you're looking at. I have jokingly suggested that our furniture mixes well with antiques and Episcopalians. Despite efforts to the contrary, I suspect we will remain a small company. You will not read about us in the Wall Street Journal and regretfully, I will not leave millions to my alma mater nor anyone else.

Looking back over the past thirty years, several impressions come to mind. The first is that I have been lucky. I've had great support from my family, particularly when we made money. I have had wonderful employees and still do, despite my shortcomings. The second is that I have been fortunate to have good, long-lasting relationships with my customers. The third is that my suppliers have stuck with me in bad times and good despite my small size, and like many small business owners, I have yet to meet a banker who knowingly took a risk.

Through all this, it occurs to me that the secret to life is being happy at eight-thirty in the morning. I look forward to the next thirty years."

WRIGHT TABLE CO.
PO Box 518
Morganton, NC 28680

Tel: 828-437-2766
Fax: 828-437-1915

Acknowledgements

In surveying several hundred industry experts, I was both surprised and very moved by how they responded to questions about the elements that create the perfect home. They were articulate, personal and very passionate in their answers. I particularly want to thank the following contributors to *The Perfect Home*:

Sally Altizer, Designer
John Aves, Managing Director
Philip Behrens, Designer
Richard Bennington, High Point University
G. Michael Black, Designer
Carrie Bleile, VP Merchandising
Don Bogish, Designer
Jackie Brezney, Designer
Mario Buatta, Interior Designer
Mary Cowan, Decorative Painter
Vaida Daukantas, Designer
Michael Delgaudio, Designer
James DeMarco, ASFD
James Dipersia, Vice President ASFD
Sandra Dollard, Interior Design Specialist
Leatrice Eiseman, Color Consultant/Author/Speaker
Leonard Eisen, Designer
Karl D. Felperin, ASFD
Robert L. Ficks Jr, Special Projects
Peter Glen, Motivational Speaker
Shirley Goff, ASFD
D. Michael Gohman, Designer
Sandra Goodall, Feng Shui Consultant
Howard Greenstein, Furniture Designer
Carl Grohs, Jr., ASFD, Consultant
Steve Hodges, Furniture Designer
Kathy Ireland, Lifestyle Designer
Alexander Julian, Designer
Haig Khachatoorian, IDSA, NC State University
Z. George Kosinski, ASFD, SFIE
Larry Laslo, Designer

Rick Lee, Product Designer
Sid Lenger, Furniture Designer
Darrell G. Lowman, ASFD
Bob Mackie, Designer
Joe Mallison, Furniture Designer
Philip Martin, Marketing
John Mascheroni, Designer
Dudley Moore, Jr., Designer
Grace Murray, Designer
Christopher Natale, Designer
Mark Ochoa, Designer
Karyl Pierce Paxton, Designer
Jason E. Payton, Designer
Joe Richardson II, Furniture Manufacturer
Joe Richardson III, Furniture Designer
Joe Ruggiero, Designer
Roger Schneeman, IDSA, ASFD
Walt Shaw, Designer
Mark Singer, Designer
Jeff Smoler, ASID, ASFD
O. B. Solie, Designer
Rosanne Somerson, Rhode Island School of Design
Greta Stookey, Furniture Designer
Charles Sutton, Furniture Manufacturer
Don Taylor, Designer
Robert Tiffany, Designer
Bob Timberlake, Artist/Designer
Raymond Waites, Designer
Michael D. Warren, Designer
Dwayne Welch, Sales/Marketing
Jonathan Willis, Furniture Designer

A special acknowledgement of appreciation to Sandy Bowles, my assistant, whose organizational skills, creative talent and personal enthusiasm were an invaluable contribution to *The Perfect Home*.

Thank you,

Joe Carroll